ISBN: **978-93-343-7859-7**
First Edition – Kindle Edition

Cover design: Shashank
Editing: Shashank

Published by Shashank (Self-Published)

This is a work of nonfiction. While every effort has been made to ensure accuracy, the author and

About the Author

I'm Shashank, a final-year BCA student with a deep passion for coding and full stack development. My journey with programming hasn't been a straight line — it's been filled with moments of confusion, trial and error, and small victories that slowly connected the dots. Writing this book was my way of sharing the lessons I've learned, in plain language, the way I wish someone had explained them to me when I first started.

Full stack development grabbed my attention because it allows me to build something completely from scratch and see it come to life. The process of designing, coding, and bringing logic and creativity together is what keeps me motivated every day. Over time, I realized that the challenges I faced weren't unique — anyone starting out in coding goes through similar hurdles, from debugging frustrating errors to figuring out how different tools fit together. That perspective guided me in writing this book: I wanted it to be practical, accessible, and confidence-boosting.

When I’m not coding or studying, I enjoy exploring new technologies, experimenting with side projects, and sharing my discoveries with others. I’m constantly learning, testing, and refining my skills, and I hope this enthusiasm comes through in my writing. My goal with this book is simple — to help readers feel less lost, more empowered, and capable of taking their own coding journey forward with clarity and confidence.

I believe that learning to code isn’t just about memorizing syntax or completing tutorials — it’s about curiosity, persistence, and building real experiences that teach you how to think like a developer. If this book helps even one person navigate that path more smoothly, then everything I put into it will have been worth it.

Chapter	Title
Chapter 1	What Even *Is* Full Stack?
Chapter 2	The Tools You'll Use (And Why)
Chapter 3	Frontend Basics: HTML, CSS, and JS
Chapter 4	Digging into JavaScript
Chapter 5	Version Control with Git & GitHub
Chapter 6	Intro to Backend with Node.js
Chapter 7	Creating APIs with Express.js
Chapter 8	Databases: MongoDB and SQL
Chapter 9	Frontend Frameworks: React Basics
Chapter 10	Connecting the Dots: Full Stack Flow

Chapter 1: What Even *Is* Full Stack?

Alright, let's start with the big question:
What does "Full Stack" actually mean?

Here's the thing — when someone says they're a *Full Stack Developer*, they just mean they can build both the **front** and the **back** of a website or app.

Let's break that down.

□ Frontend = What You See

The **frontend** is the part of a website or app that you actually look at and interact with — the buttons, the menus, the text, the colours, the layout. Basically, everything that shows up on your screen.

If you've ever used a form, clicked "Submit", or watched a popup appear on a website — that's frontend stuff.

Tools used here:
(We'll dive deeper into these later)

- HTML – structure
- CSS – style
- JavaScript – behaviour (like button clicks or animations)

⚙️ Backend = What Happens Behind the Scenes

The **backend** is the behind-the-curtain part — stuff you don't see, but it's doing all the real work.

When you sign in to a website and your name pops up, that's the backend checking who you are. When you search for something, it's the backend that finds your result. When you post a photo, the backend stores it somewhere.

The backend handles:

- Saving data
- Checking passwords
- Talking to other services
- Sending and receiving information

🧱 So What's the "Stack"?

The word **stack** just means the **layers** of technology that work together. Like stacking building blocks: one tool sits on top of another to make the whole thing run.

A **Full Stack Developer** understands and can build with *all the blocks* — both the frontend and the backend.

👩‍💻👨‍💻 Why Be a Full Stack Developer?

Because it means you're not stuck doing just one part — you can build the whole thing from start to finish. You become more independent, more flexible, and more valuable if you ever work with a team or freelance.

It’s kind of like being able to cook the entire meal, instead of just making the salad or only handling dessert.

□ But Do You Need to Know *Everything*?

Nope. Not all at once, at least.

You learn it bit by bit. You start with one side — usually the frontend — and then slowly add the backend skills. This book is going to guide you through it, one step at a time.

□ Frontend + Backend = Full Stack

Once you can build the parts you see (frontend) and the parts that work in the background (backend), and make them talk to each other — that's full stack development.

You’ll be able to create:

- Your own websites and apps
- User sign-up and login systems
- Project dashboards
- Blogs, stores, games — anything really

Final Thoughts for This Chapter

So, in plain terms:

A **Full Stack Developer** is just someone who can build both the outside *and* inside of an app or website.

You don't need to be a genius. You don't need to know everything on day one. You just need to start.

And you already have — by reading this.

Let's keep going.

Chapter 2: The Tools You'll Use (And Why)

Okay — now that you know what Full Stack is, the next step is understanding *what* tools you'll actually use to build things.

Don't worry, you don't need a hundred different apps or some supercomputer.

Just a handful of simple tools that make your life a lot easier.

Let’s go through them one by one, with plain English explanations of what they do and why they matter.

□ 1. Your Code Editor (Where You Write Stuff)

Think of a code editor like Microsoft Word — but for writing code.

Most people use **VS Code** (short for Visual Studio Code). It's free, easy to use, and helps you spot mistakes as you type.

Why it matters:
This is where you'll write every bit of your website or app. It's like your workshop.

You'll use it to:

- Write HTML, CSS, JavaScript
- Build your backend code
- Run your code and test stuff

✅ **Download tip**: Just Google "VS Code" and download it from the official site. Done.

□ 2. Your Browser (Where You See the Result)

When you build something, you want to *see* how it looks, right?

That's where your browser comes in. Chrome, Firefox, Safari — any of them work. Most people use **Google**

Chrome because it has great developer tools.

Why it matters:

- You use it to *see* your project
- You can right-click → "Inspect" to test and tweak your code live
- You'll check if your site works on different screen sizes

It's your mirror — showing you what the world will see.

🖫 3. HTML, CSS and JavaScript (The Frontend Trio)

These are the three basic building blocks of any website:

- **HTML** – adds the content
  (Think: text, buttons, images)
- **CSS** – styles the content
  (Think: colours, fonts, layout)
- **JavaScript** – makes things interactive
  (Think: clicking a button does something)

Why they matter:
This is how you build what users *see* and *use*. You'll use these three languages in nearly every project.

□ 4. Git and GitHub (For Saving and Sharing Your Work)

Let's say you're working on a project. You try something new, but it breaks everything. Oops.

Git helps you **go back in time** and undo changes. It tracks your work like checkpoints in a video game.

And GitHub? That's just a website where you can **store** your projects online and share them with others.

Why it matters:

- You won't lose your work
- You can experiment freely without breaking stuff forever
- You can work with others easily

Think of Git like "Save Game" for coding.

⚙️ 5. Node.js (For Running Code on the Backend)

Node.js lets you run JavaScript *outside* the browser — on your computer or server. This means you can use JavaScript to build the backend too.

Why it matters:
It's the engine that powers your

backend. It can handle user sign-ups, send messages, store data, and more.

With Node.js, you can use one language (JavaScript) for both frontend and backend. That's a big deal.

🚀 6. Express.js (For Creating Servers and APIs)

Express is a tool that works *with* Node.js to help you build web servers — which basically means: your project can respond when people visit it.

Example:
Someone clicks “Sign Up” → Your server (built with Express) handles the request.

Why it matters:
It’s simple, fast, and makes backend work way easier.

□ 7. Databases (For Saving Information)

Let's say someone signs up on your website. Where do you save their name, email, and password?

That's what databases are for.

There are two main kinds we'll focus on:

- **MongoDB** – good for storing flexible, messy data

- **SQL (like MySQL or PostgreSQL)** – good for structured, clean data

Why they matter:
Any app that stores user data, messages, posts, photos — all of it uses a database.

⚛️ 8. React (A Tool to Build Frontend Apps Faster)

React helps you build big websites or apps without going crazy.

Instead of repeating yourself a million times, you break your site into *components* (reusable pieces like a button or a menu). You write them once and reuse them anywhere.

Why it matters:

- Makes big projects easier to manage
- Used in most real-world jobs and projects
- Helps your site feel fast and modern

📦 9. Package Managers (For Adding Extra Features)

When you build projects, you'll often want to add things that someone else already built — like a login system, or animations.

Instead of writing everything from scratch, you can install packages using a tool like **npm** (Node Package Manager).

Why it matters:
You save time. You use tools that

professionals also use. You don't reinvent the wheel.

□ 10. Testing Tools (To Check if Things Work)

You'll later learn how to test your code to make sure it doesn't break. This is like proofreading your writing — checking for mistakes.

Tools like:

- Jest (for JavaScript)

- React Testing Library (for React apps)

Don’t worry if this sounds advanced — we’ll get to it when the time’s right.

□ 11. Deployment Tools (To Put Your App Online)

Once your project is ready, you’ll want to share it with the world.

Tools like:

- **Netlify** (for frontend sites)
- **Vercel**
- **Render**
- **Heroku** (for backend stuff)

Why it matters:
Because what's the point of building something if no one can use it?

Final Thoughts for This Chapter

You don't need to learn all of these at once. This book will walk you through each one — when you need it, why you need it, and how to use it.

But now you've got the big picture.

These tools aren't here to make life hard — they're here to make building things easier, faster, and more fun.

You're learning the toolbox of a modern builder.

Let's move on and start actually using them.

Chapter 3: Frontend Basics — HTML, CSS, and JavaScript

So now that you know what tools you'll be using, it's time to actually build something.

We start with the **frontend** — the part of a website or app that users see and interact with. This chapter covers the three building blocks of every website:

- **HTML**
- **CSS**
- **JavaScript**

You'll use these together all the time, so it's important to understand what each one does and how they work as a team.

▮ What is HTML?

HTML stands for **HyperText Markup Language**. Yeah, that sounds fancy. But here's what it really means:

HTML is how you tell the browser what's on the page.

It's the bones of the site. You use it to:

- Add text

- Create headings
- Show images
- Make buttons, links, forms, and more

Example:

```
<h1>Hello, world!</h1>
<p>This is my first
website.</p>
<img src="cat.jpg"
alt="A cute cat">
```

That code would show a big heading, a line of text, and a picture of a cat.

Think of HTML as the structure. Like walls, doors, and windows in a house.

✹ What is CSS?

CSS stands for **Cascading Style Sheets**.

CSS is how you make the page look good.

You use it to:

- Add colours
- Change fonts
- Control layout and spacing
- Make things responsive (work on phones and tablets)

Example:

```
h1 {
```

```
  color: blue;
  font-size: 36px;
}
```

That would make your `<h1>` heading big and blue.

If HTML is the structure, **CSS is the paint, furniture, and decorations**.

You can write CSS in a separate file (like `style.css`) and link it to your HTML, or write it directly inside your HTML.

✨ What is JavaScript?

Now the fun part.

JavaScript makes your site *do* things.

Buttons that actually work, popups, menus that slide open, forms that check for errors — that's all JavaScript.

It brings your site to life.

Example:

```
document.querySelector(
"button").addEventListe
ner("click", function()
{
  alert("You clicked
the button!");
});
```

That code makes a button show a message when clicked.

If HTML is the structure, and CSS is the design, **JavaScript is the brain**.

✨ How They Work Together

Here's the flow:

1. **HTML** adds the content
2. **CSS** makes it look good

3. **JavaScript** adds behaviour and logic

Imagine you're building a car:

- HTML is the frame
- CSS is the paint job and interior
- JavaScript is the engine

You need all three if you want to build something people can use.

🎨 How to Practice This Stuff

The best way to learn frontend basics is to build small things:

- A personal homepage
- A simple form
- A to-do list app

You don't need to wait until you "know everything". Just start. Make mistakes. Fix them. That's how real learning works.

Use your code editor (like VS Code) and your browser. Write some HTML. Add some CSS. Try a little JavaScript.

Start small. But start.

Final Thoughts for This Chapter

These three languages are the foundation of everything you'll build on the frontend.

You'll learn new tools and libraries later (like React), but they all build *on top of* these three. If you get comfortable with HTML, CSS, and JavaScript, the rest becomes much easier.

You now know what the frontend is made of.

Next: we dig deeper into JavaScript, because that's where a lot of the magic happens.

Chapter 4: Digging into JavaScript

Alright, time to roll up your sleeves. This chapter is all about **JavaScript** — the language that makes your website do more than just sit there looking pretty.

You already know it makes things interactive. But now we'll actually dig into how it works, what it looks like, and how you can start writing real logic into your pages.

Don’t worry if it feels weird at first. JavaScript is just a set of instructions you give your browser: "When this happens, do that."

□ What Can JavaScript Do?

- Show messages to the user
- React when someone clicks a button
- Change what’s on the page without reloading it
- Get data from other websites (more on that later)

- Store information (like usernames)

Basically: **JavaScript is what makes your app feel alive.**

✍️ Writing Your First JavaScript

You can write JavaScript in a `<script>` tag inside your HTML file, or in a separate `.js` file.

Here’s a simple example:

```
<button>Click me</button>
<script>

document.querySelector("bu
tton").addEventListener("c
lick", function() {
    alert("You clicked the
button!");
  });
</script>
```

When someone clicks the button, a little popup message appears. That’s it. That’s JavaScript doing its job.

JavaScript Basics

Let's go over the building blocks.

1. Variables

Variables store information. Like a box with a label.

```
let name = "Alex";
let age = 30;
```

2. Functions

Functions are reusable bits of code. You run them when you need them.

```
function greet() {
  console.log("Hello!");
}

greet();
```

3. Events

Events are how your page knows something happened — like a click or a key press.

```
document.querySelector("bu
tton").addEventListener("c
lick", function() {
  console.log("Button was
clicked");
});
```

4. Conditionals

These let your code make decisions.

```
let age = 18;
if (age >= 18) {
  console.log("You can
enter.");
} else {
```

```
  console.log("Sorry,
you're too young.");
}
```

5. Loops

Loops let you do the same thing multiple times.

```
for (let i = 0; i < 5;
i++) {
  console.log("Number: " +
i);
}
```

□ Where Does JavaScript Run?

JavaScript runs **in the browser**. Every modern browser has a built-in JavaScript engine. So when you open a webpage, your browser reads the HTML, applies the CSS, and runs the JavaScript.

You can open your browser's **DevTools** (usually by pressing `F12` or right-clicking and choosing "Inspect") and look under the "Console" tab. That's where JavaScript lives.

Try this right now:

```
console.log("Hello from
the console!");
```

□□ DOM: JavaScript + HTML

JavaScript can interact with the HTML on your page using something called the **DOM** (Document Object Model).

Don't let the name scare you. It just means: JavaScript can find elements in your HTML and change them.

Example:

```
<p id="message">Hello!</p>
<script>

document.getElementById("m
essage").textContent =
"New message here!";
</script>
```

Now the paragraph will say something different. Boom. Dynamic content.

🎓 Practice Ideas

Want to get better at JavaScript? Build small stuff.

- A button that changes text
- A simple calculator
- A light/dark mode switch
- A counter that goes up and down

Keep things tiny. Play around. The goal isn't to memorise, it's to understand by doing.

Final Thoughts for This Chapter

JavaScript is everywhere. You'll keep seeing it in every part of this book.

You don't need to master it overnight. But getting comfortable with variables, functions, events, and DOM changes will give you a huge head start.

JavaScript turns your static website into an actual app.

Next up: let's talk about **Git and GitHub**, so you don't lose all this great work.

Chapter 5: Version Control with Git & GitHub

Let's talk about saving your work the smart way.

If you're just building small things, you might save files like this:

- `index.html`
- `index-final.html`
- `index-final-FINAL.html`
- `index-fixed-FINAL-v2.html`

Sound familiar? We've all done it. But here's the thing:

There's a better way. And it's called **Git**.

▙ What is Git?

Git is a tool that keeps track of **every change** you make to your code. It remembers what you did, when you did it, and even lets you go back to earlier versions.

Think of it like a magical undo button that works across your entire project.

Made a mistake? Roll back.
Trying something risky? Make a copy (called a branch).
Working with a team? Everyone can see and merge each other's changes.

🔑 What is GitHub?

GitHub is a website where you can **store your Git projects online**.

You can:

- Keep backups of your work
- Share projects with others
- Work with teammates on the same codebase
- Show off your work to future employers

Git = the tool on your computer.
GitHub = the place in the cloud where your Git projects live.

🎮 Basic Git Workflow

Here's how you normally work with Git:

1. **Create a new Git repo** (repository = project)
2. Make some changes in your code
3. **Add** those changes to be tracked
4. **Commit** those changes (save a snapshot)
5. Push them to **GitHub** (optional, but useful)

In real life, that looks like this:

```
git init                        #
Start tracking this folder
with Git
git add .                       #
Add all files to be
tracked
git commit -m "First
commit"   # Save the
snapshot
git push                        #
Send it to GitHub (if set
up)
```

📁 Repositories (Repos)

A **repo** is just a project folder that Git is tracking.

You can have:

- One repo per project
- Many branches in each repo (for different versions or experiments)

You can create repos locally on your machine, or directly on GitHub.

□ Commits

Every time you make a change and want to save your progress, you make a **commit**.

Think of it like saving a checkpoint in a game.

```
git commit -m "Added login form"
```

The `-m` means "message". You leave a quick note about what you changed.

🔗 Connecting Git to GitHub

1. Create a repo on GitHub (it gives you a link)
2. In your terminal:

```
git remote add origin
https://github.com/yournam
e/your-repo.git
git push -u origin main
```

Now Git knows where to send your code.

From now on, you just run:

```
git add .
git commit -m "your
message"
git push
```

🎓 Why Learn Git Early?

- You won’t lose your code
- You’ll get used to working like a pro
- It’s required for almost every development job
- You can build a public portfolio (GitHub profile)

And once you get the hang of it, it feels natural. Like saving your game after every level.

💡 Tips

- Commit often. Don't wait until you've changed everything.
- Write clear commit messages.
- Use branches for new features or experiments.
- Push to GitHub regularly — backups are your friend.

Final Thoughts for This Chapter

Git is your project's memory. GitHub is your online backup (and bragging rights).

You don't need to learn every advanced feature now. Just get used to making commits and pushing them to GitHub.

It'll save your skin more than once.

Next: let's finally dive into **backend development** with **Node.js**. Time to make your app do more than just sit there.

Chapter 6: Intro to Backend with Node.js

Until now, everything you built ran in the browser. The frontend. But real-world apps also need a **backend** — the part that runs on a server, handles data, and responds to users.

And that's where **Node.js** comes in.

💻 What is Node.js?

Node.js is a tool that lets you run JavaScript **outside the browser**. That means you can build your server using the same language you already know.

Instead of only using JavaScript for buttons and menus, now you can use it to:

- Save and read data
- Handle logins and passwords
- Build APIs (we'll explain those soon)

- Talk to databases
- Send data to your frontend

With Node.js, JavaScript becomes a full stack language.

⚡ Setting Up Node.js

To use Node.js:

1. Go to https://nodejs.org and download it
2. Open your terminal
3. Type:

```
node -v
```

If you see a version number, it’s installed.

□ Your First Node Script

Create a file called `app.js`:

```
console.log("Hello from Node!");
```

In your terminal, run:

```
node app.js
```

It should print that message in the terminal. That’s Node running JavaScript outside the browser.

🔢 Why Use Node for the Backend?

- It’s fast
- It’s lightweight
- It uses JavaScript (so you don’t need to learn a new language)
- It works great with tools like Express, MongoDB, and others

Big companies use Node.js for real apps. You're learning tools people actually use.

📁 Node Projects

When you build a Node app, you usually:

1. Create a project folder
2. Run `npm init` to set it up
3. Write your backend logic in `.js` files

`npm` is a package manager that lets you install extra tools and libraries. You'll use it a lot.

Final Thoughts for This Chapter

Node.js is the foundation of the backend side of your full stack journey. You now know:

- What it is
- Why it matters
- How to write and run simple Node code

Next, we’ll use **Express.js** to actually respond to users and build APIs. Let’s go.

Chapter 7: Creating APIs with Express.js

Alright, so Node can run JavaScript on the backend. But building everything from scratch in Node would get messy fast.

That's why we use **Express.js** — a lightweight tool that helps you build web servers quickly and easily.

□ What is an API?

An **API** (Application Programming Interface) is just a way for your app to **send and receive data**.

Example:

- User signs in → your app sends a request to the backend

- Backend checks if the user exists → sends a response

That communication? That's an API call.

With Express.js, you can build those APIs yourself.

✨ Setting Up Express

In your project folder:

```
npm init -y
```

```
npm install express
```

Then create `server.js`:

```
const express =
require("express");
const app = express();

app.get("/", (req, res) =>
{
  res.send("Hello from
Express!");
});

app.listen(3000, () => {
```

```
  console.log("Server is running on port 3000");
});
```

Run it:

```
node server.js
```

Then open `http://localhost:3000` in your browser. You should see the message.

That’s your first API route!

📝 What's Happening Here?

- `express()` creates the app
- `app.get("/")` sets up a route (what happens when someone visits /)
- `res.send()` sends a response
- `app.listen()` starts the server

This is the base of every backend app you'll build.

Real Uses for Express

- Making login/signup forms work
- Building your own REST APIs
- Sending and receiving JSON data
- Handling forms
- Serving frontend files (like HTML, CSS, and JS)

Express does the boring setup for you so you can focus on writing your app.

□ What is JSON?

JSON stands for **JavaScript Object Notation**. It's just a way to format data.

```
{
  "name": "Alex",
  "age": 25
}
```

This is how data gets sent between frontend and backend. You'll be using it all the time.

Final Thoughts for This Chapter

You now have:

- A working backend using Node
- A simple Express server
- Your first route sending back data

Coming up next: **Databases**. Because now you need somewhere to store all that data users are sending you.

Chapter 8: Databases - MongoDB and SQL

Now that your app can handle requests and send responses, you need a place to **store data**.
That’s what a **database** is for.

Let’s break it down.

📂 What is a Database?

A database is like a smart filing cabinet. Instead of saving data in files manually, you use a database to:

- Store user info (names, emails, passwords)
- Keep track of tasks, posts, orders, anything
- Search and update data efficiently

There are two major types:

- **SQL databases** (like MySQL, PostgreSQL)
- **NoSQL databases** (like MongoDB)

🔢 SQL: Structured Data

SQL databases use **tables**, kind of like Excel sheets.

- Rows = records
- Columns = fields (name, email, etc.)

You write commands using SQL language, like:

```
SELECT * FROM users WHERE
email =
'someone@example.com';
```

SQL is great when your data has clear structure and relationships.

□ NoSQL: Flexible Data

MongoDB is a **NoSQL** database. It stores data in **JSON-like format**, called documents.

Example:

```
{
  "name": "Tina",
  "email":
"tina@example.com",
  "isAdmin": false
}
```

This is great when:

- Your data doesn’t always follow the same structure
- You want to move fast
- You're using JavaScript (Mongo works well with Node)

✨ MongoDB in Node Projects

You can use a tool like **Mongoose** to connect MongoDB to your Node.js app. Example:

```
npm install mongoose
```

Then in your server:

```
const mongoose =
require("mongoose");

mongoose.connect("mongodb:
//localhost:27017/myapp")
  .then(() =>
console.log("DB
connected"))
  .catch(err =>
console.log(err));
```

Now your app can read and write data.

🎓 Which One Should You Learn?

Both.

- MongoDB is easier to get started with (especially with Node + Express)
- SQL is powerful and used everywhere

Learn MongoDB first to build quickly, then explore SQL once you're comfortable.

Final Thoughts for This Chapter

You now know the basics of databases, how they store your data, and the difference between SQL and NoSQL.

Next: let's jump back to the frontend and look at something powerful: **React**.

Chapter 9: Frontend Frameworks - React Basics

Writing JavaScript to update the DOM (your page) manually gets messy fast. That's why frameworks like **React** exist — they make it easier to build fast, interactive user interfaces.

💡 What is React?

React is a **JavaScript library** built by Facebook for building user interfaces.

With React, you build small reusable pieces of UI called **components**.

Example:

```
function Welcome() {
```

```
  return <h1>Hello!</h1>;
}
```

React handles updating the page when things change, so you don't have to manually mess with the DOM.

📅 Setting Up React

Easiest way to start:

```
npx create-react-app my-
app
cd my-app
```

```
npm start
```

This gives you a ready-to-go React app with everything set up.

🔒 How React Works

- You write **components** (functions that return UI)
- React turns them into real HTML
- When data changes, React updates only what's needed

⚖️ JSX = JavaScript + HTML

React uses a special syntax called **JSX**:

```
const name = "Tina";
return <h1>Hello,
{name}</h1>;
```

You can write HTML and JS together — cleaner and easier to manage.

React Component Example

```
function Button() {
```

```
  return <button>Click
Me</button>;
}
```

You can reuse this button anywhere in your app.

⚛️ Props and State

- **Props** = data you pass into components
- **State** = data inside a component that can change

Example with state:

```
import { useState } from
"react";

function Counter() {
  const [count, setCount]
= useState(0);

  return (
    <div>
      <p>{count}</p>
      <button onClick={()
=> setCount(count +
1)}>Add</button>
```

```
    </div>
  );
}
```

Final Thoughts for This Chapter

React makes building dynamic frontends much easier.
You now know:

- What React is
- How to make components
- What JSX, props, and state are

You're getting closer to building real, powerful apps that talk to the backend and handle user input.

Next chapter: bringing it all together into a full stack flow.

Chapter 10: Connecting the Dots - Full Stack Flow

You've now seen the frontend (HTML, CSS, JS, React) and the backend (Node, Express, MongoDB). This chapter is about how they actually **work together**.

Let's connect the dots.

□ The Big Picture

A full stack app usually works like this:

1. User visits a page (React handles this)
2. They click a button or submit a form
3. That triggers an API call to the backend (Express)
4. The backend processes the request and talks to the database (MongoDB)
5. It sends data back to the frontend
6. React updates what the user sees

That back-and-forth flow is what makes your app feel alive.

□□ Example Flow: Sign Up

1. User fills out sign-up form
2. You send a `POST` request to `/api/signup`
3. Backend saves the user in the database
4. It sends back a response like `Signup successful`
5. React shows a success message or redirects to another page

It’s all just requests and responses.
Your job is to handle them cleanly.

□ Frontend <-> Backend

They talk using **fetch** or **Axios** (tools to send requests from the browser).

React example:

```
fetch("/api/users")
  .then(res => res.json())
  .then(data =>
console.log(data));
```

This calls the backend and logs the response.

□ Why This Matters

You're not building random parts anymore.
You're building **a system**:

- Frontend handles display and user input
- Backend handles logic and data
- Database keeps everything safe and permanent

Once you get this flow, everything clicks.

Final Thoughts for This Chapter

You now understand how a full stack app flows:

- Requests come in
- Backend handles it
- Database stores it
- Frontend reacts

Next: how to make sure it looks good on **every device**.

Chapter 11: Responsive Design That Works Everywhere

Users aren't just on laptops. They're on phones, tablets, giant monitors. Your app needs to **look good and work properly** everywhere.
That's what responsive design is about.

💻📱 Why Responsive Design Matters

Imagine a form that looks great on desktop but is broken on a phone.

That’s a problem. You don’t want people pinching and zooming to use your app.

Good responsive design =

- Easy to read on small screens
- Buttons and inputs that aren’t cramped
- Layouts that adjust smoothly

🌈 CSS Media Queries

Media queries let you write CSS that only applies on certain screen sizes.

Example:

```
@media (max-width: 600px)
{
  .nav {
    flex-direction:
column;
  }
}
```

This changes the layout when the screen is smaller than 600px wide.

□□ Flexible Layouts

Use things like:

- **Percentages** instead of fixed widths (so things scale)
- **Flexbox** and **Grid** (for auto-adjusting layouts)
- **max-width** instead of just width

That way your site isn't locked to one screen size.

☕ Mobile-First Design

Start with mobile layout first, then add styles for bigger screens.
Why?

- It forces you to focus on the essentials
- It usually ends up cleaner and simpler

Example:

```
/* Start simple */
.card { width: 100%;
padding: 1rem; }

/* Add this later for
bigger screens */
@media (min-width: 768px)
{
  .card { width: 50%; }
}
```

□ Bonus Tools

- Use **Chrome DevTools** to test different screen sizes
- Use **CSS frameworks** like Tailwind or Bootstrap (they have built-in responsive classes)
- Try **rem** and **em** units for scalable fonts

Final Thoughts for This Chapter

Responsive design isn't about making things fancy. It's about making sure everyone can actually use your app, no matter where they are or what they're using.

You now know:

- How to write responsive CSS
- What tools to use
- Why designing for mobile first is smart

Next, let's deal with something super common: **forms and user input**.

Chapter 12: Handling Forms and User Input

Your app needs to talk to real people. That means handling input: forms, buttons, fields, all of it.

Let’s break it down.

Forms in HTML

A basic form looks like this:

```
<form>
  <input type="text"
placeholder="Your name" />
  <button
type="submit">Send</button
>
</form>
```

You use inputs to collect things like:

- Names
- Emails

- Passwords
- Comments, messages, etc.

Handling Forms in React

In React, you usually control the input using **state**.

Example:

```
function MyForm() {
  const [name, setName] =
useState("");
```

```
  const handleSubmit = (e)
=> {
    e.preventDefault();
    console.log("Submitted
name:", name);
  };

  return (
    <form
onSubmit={handleSubmit}>
      <input value={name}
onChange={(e) =>
setName(e.target.value)}
/>
```

```
        <button
type="submit">Submit</butt
on>
      </form>
    );
}
```

❌ Preventing Page Reload

React doesn't want to reload the page every time you submit a form.
Use `e.preventDefault()` to stop that.

✅ Validating Input

Check the values before sending them off:

- Are required fields filled?
- Is the email valid?
- Is the password long enough?

You can do this with plain JS before submitting.

Final Thoughts for This Chapter

Forms are the bridge between your user and your app. Mastering them means you can start capturing real data and interactions. Get the hang of managing state and validating input, and you're already ahead.

Chapter 13: User Authentication - Sign Up & Log In

Now that you can collect user input, let's do something useful: **sign up and log in**.

🔑 The Basics of Auth

Authentication = verifying who someone is.

- **Sign Up** = create an account (store name, email, password)
- **Log In** = check if email + password match existing user

How It Works

1. User submits signup form
2. You send a `POST` request to `/api/signup`
3. Backend saves user in DB (with **hashed password**, never plain text)
4. User gets logged in automatically or redirected to login page

Logging in is similar:

- Send email + password to `/api/login`
- Backend checks if they match
- If yes, backend returns a token or session info

□ Sessions vs Tokens

- **Sessions** = info stored on server (common in traditional apps)
- **Tokens** = info stored on frontend (usually with JWTs in modern apps)

🔒 Security Notes

- Always **hash passwords** with something like bcrypt
- Never store plain text passwords
- Protect routes that need login (backend should check if user is allowed)

Final Thoughts for This Chapter

Authentication is about trust. If users can't safely log in and out, the rest doesn't matter. Lock it down, keep it secure, and make the process smooth.

Chapter 14: APIs, Fetching Data & Error Handling

Your app won't just send data — it needs to **get data too**.
That means calling APIs.

🔍 Fetching Data in React

Use `fetch()` to get data from the backend:

```
js
CopyEdit
useEffect(() => {
  fetch("/api/users")
    .then(res =>
res.json())
    .then(data =>
setUsers(data));
}, []);
```

You use `useEffect` so the call happens when the component loads.

Handling Errors

Always add `.catch()` to handle errors:

```
js
CopyEdit
fetch("/api/something")
  .then(res => res.json())
  .then(data =>
doSomething(data))
```

```
  .catch(err =>
console.error("Oops:",
err));
```

Or better: use `try/catch` with async/await.

□ Showing Loading + Error States

Good UI tells the user what's happening:

- Show a spinner or "Loading..." while data is coming

- Show a message if something goes wrong

✅ Final Thoughts for This Chapter

APIs are your connection to everything beyond your app.
If you can fetch data, show it right, and handle when things break, you're thinking like a real dev.

Chapter 15: Working with JSON and External APIs

Most APIs (including your own) send and receive **JSON**.
It's the format everyone agrees on.

■ What is JSON?

JSON = JavaScript Object Notation

It looks like this:

```json
json
CopyEdit
{
  "name": "Luna",
  "age": 25
}
```

Easy to read, easy to parse in JavaScript.

□ External APIs

You can also call public APIs, like:

- Weather data
- GitHub user info
- News, stock prices, etc.

Example:

```
js
CopyEdit
fetch("https://api.github.
com/users/yourusername")
  .then(res => res.json())
  .then(data =>
console.log(data));
```

🚀 Use JSON in Your Own API

Your own backend will also send/receive JSON:

```
js
CopyEdit
res.json({ success: true,
user });
```

And the frontend will read it like:

```
js
CopyEdit
.then(res => res.json())
```

✅ Final Thoughts for This Chapter

JSON is the universal language of web data.
If you can read it, send it, and build around it, you can integrate with pretty much anything.

Chapter 16: State Management in React

By now, you've used `useState` in React. But when your app grows, juggling state across multiple components gets tricky.
Let's fix that.

□ What is State Management?

State = the current data your app is working with.

Managing it = keeping track of what changes and where — without everything breaking.

□ Local State with `useState`

Still useful for small things:

```jsx
jsx
CopyEdit
const [count, setCount] =
useState(0);
```

But if you need to share that count between components, it gets messy.

🏠 Lifting State Up

If two components need the same state, move it up to their common parent.

```
jsx
CopyEdit
// Parent holds the state
const [value, setValue] =
useState("hello");
```

```
// Pass it down as props
to both children
```

It works, but as your app grows, you'll get "prop drilling" — passing props through multiple levels just to get data where you need it.

□ Context API

React's built-in solution for global-ish state:

```
jsx
```

```
CopyEdit
const ThemeContext =
React.createContext();
```

Wrap your app in a provider:

```
jsx
CopyEdit
<ThemeContext.Provider
value={value}>
  <App />
</ThemeContext.Provider>
```

Then you can read the value from any component with:

```jsx
useContext(ThemeContext)
```

⚙️ Tools Like Redux (Optional)

If Context isn’t enough, tools like Redux or Zustand give you more control.

But don’t jump into them too early — they add complexity.

✅ Final Thoughts This for Chapter

State is what makes your app feel alive. Whether it's just toggling a menu or syncing data between views, managing state cleanly makes your code easier to read and your app more reliable.

Chapter 17: Building a Real-World Project (Part 1)

Let's build something real using everything so far — frontend, backend, database, forms, auth, and state.

□ Pick Your Stack

Example stack:

- React for frontend
- Node.js + Express for backend

- MongoDB for database

📌 Project Idea

Let's build a simple **task manager**:

- Users can sign up / log in
- Create, edit, and delete tasks
- Mark tasks as complete

□ App Flow

1. User signs up or logs in

2. They land on their dashboard
3. Dashboard shows their tasks
4. They can add a task (form)
5. Backend saves it to DB
6. UI updates with new data

□ Features to Start With

- Auth (sign up, login)
- Task list (fetch from backend)
- Add new task (form + POST request)
- Delete task (button + DELETE request)

- Mark complete (toggle with PUT or PATCH)

□ Start Small

Don’t try to build everything at once. Start with sign-up + login, then show a list of dummy tasks. Once that’s working, connect it to the backend.

✅ Final Thoughts for This Chapter

This is where it starts to feel real. You're not just learning concepts — you're stitching them together into something useful. It’s messy, but that’s part of the process. Build, test, break it, fix it, repeat.

Chapter 18: Building a Real-World Project (Part 2)

Now we take your project further. The skeleton is there — let's flesh it out.

✏️ Editing Tasks

Add an "Edit" button next to each task. When clicked:

- Turn the text into an input field
- Let user update it

- Save changes with a PUT request

📱 Make It Responsive

Use media queries or tools like Tailwind to make sure it works well on:

- Mobile
- Tablet
- Desktop

👤 Show Logged-in User

Once the user is logged in:

- Show their name or email on the page
- Maybe even let them log out with a button

🗌 Clean Up Code

Start organising your files:

- `components/`

- `pages/`
- `services/`

Break big components into smaller ones.

Handle Edge Cases

What happens when:

- API call fails?
- A user tries to delete a task that's already gone?

Show proper error messages and feedback.

✅ Final Thoughts for This Chapter

This is the polishing phase. You take your MVP (Minimum Viable Product) and make it feel like a real app. It's not about adding everything — it's about making what you have solid.

Chapter 19: Testing and Debugging Your Code

Things break. Bugs happen. Good developers know how to find and fix them.

🐞 Console Logs

Still your best friend:

```
js
CopyEdit
```

```
console.log("Task data:", task);
```

Use it to check what data is being passed and where things go wrong.

🔍 Chrome DevTools

Inspect elements, watch API calls, check network requests. Learn to:

- Use the “Network” tab to check if your API is working

- See console errors and trace them back to your code

✅ Basic Manual Testing

Test your app like a user:

- Try submitting an empty form
- Try logging in with the wrong password
- Refresh pages — does state stay or break?

□ Writing Tests (Optional)

For bigger projects, you can write unit tests using:

- Jest (for JS functions)
- React Testing Library (for components)

But early on, focus more on building and debugging manually.

✅ Final Thoughts for This Chapter

Testing and debugging are how you level up. When things go wrong — and they will — your job is to figure out why, not panic. Use the tools, stay curious, and learn from every bug.

Chapter 20: Deployment – Getting Your App Online

You've built your app. It works on your machine. Great.
But now it's time to show the world.

Let's get your app online.

🚀 What Is Deployment?

Deployment means putting your app on the internet where anyone can access it — from a phone, a laptop, anywhere.

You take:

- Your **frontend code** (React)
- Your **backend server** (Node/Express)
- Your **database** (MongoDB or SQL)

And host them so they run 24/7.

□ Tools You Can Use

Frontend Hosting:

- Vercel – great for React
- Netlify – also great for static sites
- GitHub Pages – for simple frontends

Backend Hosting:

- Render
- Railway

- Heroku *(still used, but not free forever)*

Database Hosting:

- MongoDB Atlas
- PlanetScale for MySQL

☐ General Steps

1. Push your code to GitHub
2. Connect your hosting platform to your GitHub repo

3. Set up **environment variables** (like DB connection strings, secrets)
4. Deploy the frontend + backend
5. Test everything live

🔐 Don't Forget

- Never upload `.env` files or secrets to GitHub
- Set CORS properly on your backend

- Make sure errors are handled even in production

□ Things Will Break (And That's Normal)

Deployment comes with:

- CORS errors
- Build errors
- Missing environment variables
- Backend not reachable by frontend

You’ll fix them. It's just part of the game.

✅ Final Thoughts for This Chapter

Deployment is where your code becomes real. It’s not done until it’s live. When you see your project running on a public link — even with rough edges — that’s when it clicks. You made something. It works.

Conclusion: So What Now?

You've built the front end. You've wired up the backend. You've made requests, handled errors, managed state, talked to databases, and finally got your app online.

That's full stack.

But here’s the thing — you’re not *done*. You’ve just crossed the starting line.

Now you actually know enough to:

- Build your own projects
- Read docs without getting lost
- Understand how real-world apps work

- Google better, debug faster, and not freak out when things break

You don't need to memorise everything. You just need to *know what's possible* and *how to figure things out*. And now you do.

So take what you've built. Break it. Rebuild it. Add something weird. Make it yours.

That's how you get better. That's how you become a real dev.

You're already on your way.

www.ingramcontent.com/pod-product-compliance
Lightning Source LLC
Chambersburg PA
CBHW050527240926
51846CB00003B/721
9789334378597